D0773727

A Look at METAMORPHIC ROCKS

Cecelia H. Brannon

Enslow Publishing
101 W. 23rd Street
Suite 240
New York, NY 10011
USA
enslow.com

Published in 2016 by Enslow Publishing, LLC
101 W. 23rd Street, Suite 240, New York, NY 10011

Library of Congress Cataloging-in-Publication Data

Brannon, Cecelia H., author.
    A look at metamorphic rocks / Cecelia H. Brannon.
        pages cm. — (The rock cycle)
    Audience: Ages 8+
    Audience: Grades 4 to 6.
    Includes bibliographical references and index.
    ISBN 978-0-7660-7322-7 (library binding)
    ISBN 978-0-7660-7320-3 (pbk.)
    ISBN 978-0-7660-7321-0 (6-pack)
    1. Metamorphic rocks—Juvenile literature. 2. Geochemical cycles—Juvenile literature. I. Title.
    QE475.B68 2016
    552.4—dc23
                        2015029179

Printed in the United States of America

To Our Readers: We have done our best to make sure all websites in this book were active and appropriate when we went to press. However, the author and the publisher have no control over and assume no liability for the material available on those websites or any websites they may link to. Any comments or suggestions can be sent by e-mail to customerservice@enslow.com.

Photo Credits: Throughout book: Kues/Shutterstock.com (sand texture), Vladislav Gajic/Shutterstock.com (colorful rock), alexkar08/Shutterstock.com (weathered rough stone) Christine Yarusi (series logo, four-rock dingbat); cover, p. 1 Baloncici/Shutterstock.com (yellow marble),Vladislav Gajic/Shutterstock.com (dark green marble), Kriengsuk Prasroetsung/Shutterstock.com (light green marble); p. 4 Lukasz Miegoc/Shutterstock.com; p. 6 © iStockphoto.com/ Gianluca Figliola Fantini; p.7 Johan Swanepoel/Shutterstock.com; p. 9 ZeWrestler/Wikimedia Commons/Rockcycle2.jpg/public domain; p. 11 Zhukova Valentyna; p. 12 Ammit Jack/Shutterstock.com; p. 14 Kenneth Keifer/Shutterstock.com; p. 15 Designua/Shutterstock.com; p. 16 Lee Prince/Shutterstock.com; p. 17 Everett Historical/Shutterstock.com; p. 19 Ann Louise Hagevi/Shutterstock.com; p. 20 Tyler Boyes/Shutterstock.com (slate and gneiss); p. 21 Kevin Penhallow/Shutterstock.com (roofscape), Artography/Shutterstock.com (garnet schist); p. 23 © iStockphoto.com/mtreasure; p. 24 aleramo/Shutterstock.com; p. 25 www.sandatlas.org/Shutterstock.com; p. 27 MarcelClemens/Shutterstock.com (kyanite), Stellar Gems/Shutterstock.com (andalusite); p. 28 Colin D. Young/Shutterstock.com.

Contents

The Alps mountain range in Europe is made from metamorphic rock.

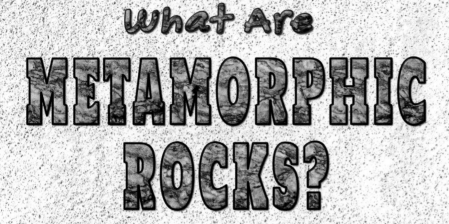

What Are METAMORPHIC ROCKS?

There are three different kinds of rock that make up Earth: igneous, sedimentary, and metamorphic. These rocks are always changing. Intense heat or pressure change igneous and sedimentary rocks into a new kind of rock—a metamorphic rock.

How Rocks Change

The rocks that make up our planet are constantly changing through a process called the rock cycle. In this process, old rocks are broken down to form new ones.

Through the rock cycle, the layers that make up our planet are always changing. The top layer

Pedra Azul ("blue stone") in Brazil is an enormous metamorphic rock. It is made of granite.

of Earth where we live is called the crust and is made of rock. Below that is a layer of hot liquid called magma, which makes up the mantle. At the center of Earth is the core, which is made of two layers. The outer core is made of melted metals, while the inner core is a solid metal ball.

6

What Are **METAMORPHIC ROCKS?**

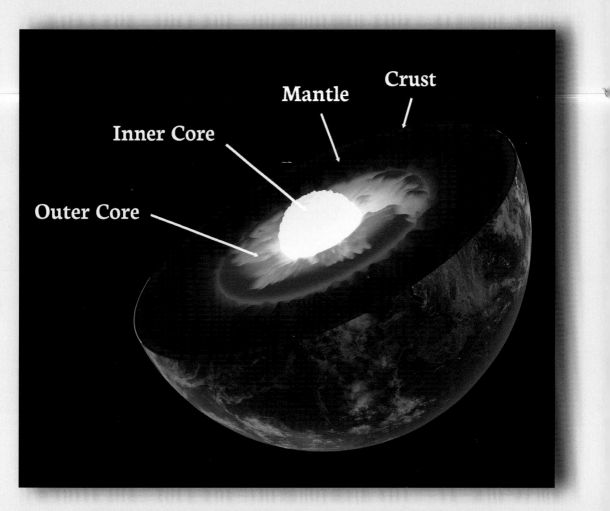

Earth is made of several layers of rock and metal.

The rock cycle begins when hot magma flows through cracks in Earth's crust. Exposed to air or water, this magma cools and hardens into igneous rocks. Through weathering and erosion, these igneous rocks wear down to create sediment. Over time and with pressure, these layers of sediment will become sedimentary rocks. More heat or pressure can cause these igneous or sedimentary rocks to change yet again, which creates metamorphic rocks.

Metamorphic rocks then break down over time and form sediment again, which creates sedimentary rocks. Or, if metamorphic rocks melt, magma is formed. The rock cycle begins again!

What Are **METAMORPHIC ROCKS?**

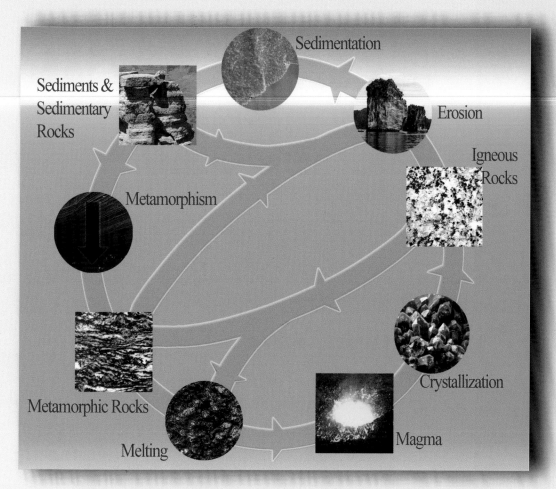

Sedimentation

Sediments & Sedimentary Rocks

Erosion

Igneous Rocks

Metamorphism

Crystallization

Metamorphic Rocks

Melting

Magma

This diagram illustrates the rock cycle. Strong heat and pressure turn igneous and sedimentary rocks into metamorphic rocks.

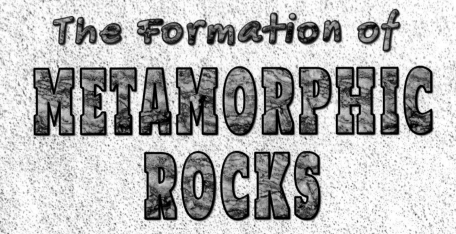

The Formation of METAMORPHIC ROCKS

Metamorphic rocks form one of two ways. One way is through the intense heat created by magma. The other way is through the enormous pressure inside Earth.

Extreme Heat

Forces inside Earth create heat. Earth's layers press down on each other and force hot magma up toward the surface. Sometimes, this magma escapes through volcanoes when they erupt. Other times, a small amount of magma pushes through a crack in Earth's crust. This is called a magma surge.

The volcanic eruption or magma surge creates an intense heat, which makes the rocks around

Much of the Rocky Mountains in the western part of the United States are made from metamorphic rocks called quartzite.

The Tungurahua volcano in Ecuador erupted in 2011.

the magma very hot. So hot, in fact, that the minerals inside the rock metamorphose, or change, to form a new kind of rock. Metamorphic rocks form when the temperature around rocks gets from 300 to 2,000° F (149 to 1,093° C).

Pressure Buildup

The layers of Earth are heavy. Imagine carrying a mountain. Then, imagine carrying several thousand mountains!

When Earth's layers press down on each other, it causes pressure to build up, which pushes rocks into one another. The rocks are under so much pressure that their minerals change to create metamorphic rocks.

When this strong pressure continues, sometimes the metamorphic rocks are pushed up and out of Earth's crust. This is how mountains are formed.

Fault Lines

The Earth's crust is not one solid piece. It consists of many large pieces called tectonic plates. These plates float on the mantle of liquid magma. Earth's surface is always moving. We cannot feel it, but we can see it. The proof is in metamorphic rocks.

Did You Know?

The Waterpocket Fold is a feature in Earth's crust in Capitol Reef National Park in Utah. It is nearly 100 miles (161 kilometers) long. You can see the layers of rocks and the amount of pressure they're under.

The Formation of METAMORPHIC ROCKS

This diagram shows Earth's plates. The major plates are named after the continents or oceans they contain.

Sometimes, the tectonic plates scrape against each other. This creates a weak spot in the crust called a fault line. When the pressure inside Earth gets too strong, the plates shift, which causes an earthquake.

Volcanoes can also form along fault lines. Magma can burst through fault lines and reach the surface. The tremendously high temperatures and stress can change the molecules in the surface rocks. Any time a rock's minerals or molecules change, it becomes a metamorphic rock.

This fault line is in Flaming Gorge, Utah.

The Formation of METAMORPHIC ROCKS

Different Types of METAMORPHIC ROCKS

There are two main categories of metamorphic rock: foliated and nonfoliated. Foliated rocks occur when pressure forces the minerals in metamorphic rocks into wavy lines, which makes the rock look layered or striped. Nonfoliated metamorphic rocks do not have the stripes that foliated rocks do.

Foliated Rocks

Foliated rocks almost look like grains in wood. The word foliated comes from the Latin word *folia*, which means "leaves."

This beach in Sweden is made of red granite, a kind of metamorphic rock.

Slate is a kind of foliated rock.

Gneiss (pronounced NICE) is a well-known foliated rock. It is formed when heat or pressure changes an igneous rock called granite. Gneiss has many stripes of color in it. These stripes take shape because the minerals in the rock separate into layers as the rock is formed.

Gneiss is one of the toughest rocks in the world.

Shale, a sedimentary rock, changes into the foliated metamorphic rock slate. Shale becomes slate when sediment in rivers and lakes becomes pressurized in low heat. Slate is very hard, but it breaks easily into flat pieces. Usually, slate is gray, but it can be black, green, blue, or even purple.

Different Types of METAMORPHIC ROCKS

Slate is often used on roofs.

Did You Know?

The minerals in schist often form a gem called garnet. Garnets are usually red, but they can also be yellow, green, pink, blue, and other colors. Garnet is often used to make jewelry. It is the birthstone of people born in January.

Slate can change into another metamorphic rock called schist. Schist forms when slate reaches a high temperature. Schist is also often used as a building material for roofs, foundations, and landscaping.

Nonfoliated Rocks

A well-known example of a nonfoliated rock is marble. Marble is created along fault lines from limestone. It is a soft stone that can easily be carved into statues and stones for building. It is usually white but can also be black, red, green, blue, gray, purple, or even pink. Impurities in the limestone that created the marble cause the different colors.

Often in ancient Rome, the colored marble was used for mosaics and floors. The different colors represented the wealth and power of the owner and the Roman empire.

Quartzite is a hard metamorphic rock. It is sometimes used to build roads. Quartzite forms when sandstone, a sedimentary rock, is changed by heat and pressure deep inside Earth. Quartzite contains quartz, a hard mineral found in sedimentary, igneous, and metamorphic rocks that makes rocks look shiny.

This is red marble with
a mineral called quartz
running through it.

The Trevi fountain in Rome, Italy, is carved from marble.

This is quartzite. It is usually white or gray, but it can be red, pink, orange, green, or blue because of impurities in the rock.

Hornfels is a type of metamorphic rock that forms when shale comes in contact with magma at temperatures from 392 to 1,472° F (200 to 800° C). Hornfels is a hard rock that comes in dark colors of gray or black. It is commonly used in building roads.

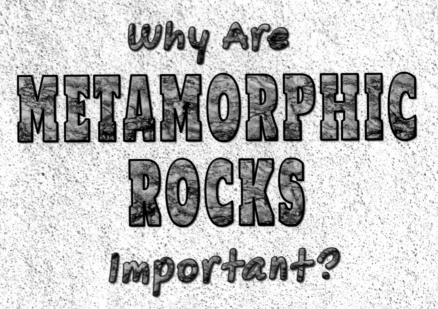

Why Are METAMORPHIC ROCKS Important?

Metamorphic rocks are very useful to people. The minerals found in these rocks can withstand high temperatures and are often used for things like insulation and electrical machinery. Metamorphic rocks are also used for buildings, roads, decoration, jewelry, and many other things.

Why Are **METAMORPHIC ROCKS** Important?

An example of a mineral in metamorphic rocks is kyanite. It is used in machinery, such as cutting tools and grinding wheels.

Andalusite is a metamorphic rock mineral used to make jewelry.

The rock ledges below the Pemaquid Point Lighthouse in Maine are mostly made up of metamorphic rocks that changed hundreds of millions of years ago.

Why Are **METAMORPHIC ROCKS** Important?

Metamorphic rocks are also an important part of Earth. Scientists study their appearance, location, and minerals to learn about the temperatures and pressures beneath Earth's crust. The rocks provide information about the changes that are occurring above and below Earth's surface.

Metamorphic rocks are part of the process that creates new rocks in the rock cycle, which has been shaping and reshaping Earth for millions of years. As long as Earth continues to exist, metamorphic rocks will keep playing their important part in the rock cycle.

Glossary

fault line—A place on Earth's surface where two plates meet.

foliated—Having to do with metamorphic rocks that have minerals in wavy lines or bands.

igneous—Having to do with a hot, liquid, underground mineral that has cooled and hardened.

magma—Hot liquid rock beneath Earth's surface.

metamorphic—Having to do with rock that has been changed by heat and heavy weight.

minerals—Natural elements that are not animals, plants, or other living things.

molecules—The smallest bits of matter possible before they can be broken down into their basic parts.

nonfoliated—Having to do with metamorphic rocks that are smooth and do not have wavy lines of minerals.

plates—The moving pieces of Earth's crust.

sediment—Mud, clay, or bits of rock carried by water.

sedimentary—Having to do with layers of stones, sand, or mud that have been pressed together to form rock.

Further Reading

BOOKS

Dee, Willa. *Unearthing Metamorphic Rocks* (Rocks: The Hard Facts). New York: PowerKids Press, 2014.

Green, Dan. *Discover More: Rocks and Minerals*. New York: Scholastic. 2013.

Spilsbury, Richard. *Metamorphic Rocks* (Earth's Rocky Past). New York: PowerKids Press, 2015.

Swanson, Jennifer. *Metamorphic Rocks* (Rocks and Minerals). Edina, Minn.: Core Library Publishing. 2014.

WEBSITES

Science Kids: Metamorphic Rock facts

sciencekids.co.nz/sciencefacts/earth/metamorphicrocks.html

Facts about metamorphic rocks.

Geology.com: Metamorphic Rocks

geology.com/rocks/metamorphic-rocks.shtml

See different types of metamorphic rocks and learn how they're made.

Windows to the Universe: Rocks and the Rock Cycle

windows2universe.org/earth/geology/rocks_intro.html

Learn about sedimentary, igneous, and metamorphic rocks in the rock cycle.

Index